GHOSTS OF ELLICOTT CITY

By Russ Noratel

Edited by

Elizabeth Noratel

Cover Designed by Vince Wilson

Copyright 2012 Russ Noratel

To: Sam
Thanks For All Your Support!
Happy Memorial Day!
Enjoy
Russ Noratel
5-27-12

CONTENTS

This book is dedicated to my mom and dad who have always supported me in everything that I do.

INTRODUCTION

I have lived in a small town just outside of Baltimore all of my life. Like any true Marylander, I enjoy steamed crabs, Natty Boh and the Orioles. I'm a history buff, and that is an easy hobby to pursue in such a historically rich state as Maryland. Paranormal Research is my passion. Ever since I was young, I've wondered if something else was out there. In my twenties, I began looking into what might lie out there in the dark.

My journey began by looking into one of Maryland's little gems called Ellicott City. In high school I had heard many stories about a great little town nestled by the Patapsco River. My friends would tell me stories of the ambiance of the town. I finally was convinced to visit Old Town Ellicott City. What I found was far beyond anything I could imagine.

The only way that I can think to describe Ellicott City is CHARM. I don't think that there is anywhere else in Maryland that can claim the same amount of history in such a small space. During my first trip to the town I was in awe of all of the historic buildings in downtown Ellicott City. As a history buff I couldn't help but imagine the town in the Civil War Era, bustling with activity. I remember venturing into a coffee house called Sarah and Desmond's along

Main Street. On that fateful day, I bought a cup of coffee and fell in love with that little town. What I didn't know as I sat in that wonderful coffee house, were the plethora of ghost stories that the town possessed. I also didn't know that I was sitting in a coffee house that had plenty of ghost stories itself.

My journey into researching the haunted side of Ellicott City has been one that I have enjoyed. I have talked to so many wonderful people that had such amazing stories and I am grateful to every one of them. I hope that you will find the same joy in reading about this town, its history and its haunts, as I have found in researching them.

Russ Noratel

A BRIEF HISTORY OF ELLICOTT CITY

Ellicott Mills (later to be named Ellicott City) was founded by the Ellicott Brothers, Andrew, Joseph and John in 1771. The three grew up as Quakers in Bucks County, Pennsylvania. They moved to Maryland to make a stake for themselves. The Ellicott Brothers had this crazy idea to grow wheat in a land that had long ago been made infertile by early tobacco farming. They purchased a rather large chunk of land and used modern farming techniques to make the ground fertile enough to raise wheat. Since the brothers knew that they would need mills to make the flour, the mills were built along the Patapsco River.

The Ellicotts experimented with various farming techniques and machinery and the town sprang up around the farms and mills. By the 1800's Ellicott Mills was well known and had a very good reputation. Other mills eventually popped up in the town over the course of the next century and the town prospered.

There were no roads in the area when the Ellicott Brothers first settled. The first major roads were built by the Ellicotts, as was (what is known today as) Route 40. The roads were built to keep the grain flowing to the Mills. The B&O Railroad was also built through the town. The land was given to the railroad by the Ellicott's because they knew that there would be vast financial rewards to having a rail-station in the town. The investments in the roads and railroad both paid off for the Ellicotts in the end.

During the civil war, the B&O railroad station in Ellicott City played a key role. The railroad was crucial in delivering much-needed union troops to the battle as well as returning the wounded and dead from the front lines. The B&O was also crucial in getting union troops to Ellicott City as southern sympathizers (the town was mostly north loyal) tried to get a steam-powered machine gun (called the Winan's Steam Gun) through town. The southerners failed to get that gun through town, the Union troops descended upon them during transport of the gun because the railroad was able to get them there in time.

Ellicott City has also experienced many catastrophes over the years. Many of these catastrophes have been due to floods. The town has flooded at least 4 times over the last 200 years. The first time was in 1780, when the Ellicotts discovered the bad side to living along a river. The Flood of 1780 swept the town away, but there was no loss of human life. Ellicott City wasn't so lucky in 1868 however. The water rose to its highest level ever and 36 people died. Hurricanes Agnes and Eloise took a crack at flooding the town as well in the 1970's.

Despite so much tragedy, the town showed its true resilience by rebuilding. The only sign of the floods that you can find today is the hash marks on the Railroad Bridge across Main Street. Each hash mark represents the height of the water during the floods from 1868 onward. With so much tragedy and such rich history, it is no wonder why there are so many ghost stories that surround this town.

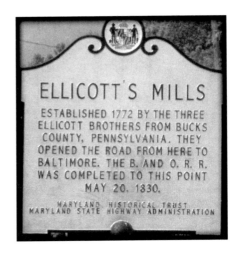

THE TIBER RIVER TAVERN

Now the Diamondback

The Tiber River Tavern is perhaps one of the most famous and actively haunted locations in Ellicott City. It is located in what were once horse stables, along

Old Columbia Pike. Though the Tavern shut down in late June 2008, the building still stands as a reminder that though businesses may come and go, the town still remains. What also remains are the stories of the lady ghost that still walks within the tavern. There are too many stories about this tavern to recount to you, so I will just stick with a few that I have heard.

During the course of my interviews with various town folk, the Tiber River Tavern came up more than once. While interviewing a former employee named Tommy, I was told that the Tavern was host to a tragedy over a century earlier. Apparently a poor girl was murdered on the top floor of the restaurant and bar. I was not able to confirm that a girl died at this location during my research however.

Tommy went on to tell me about just a few of the reported sightings of the female spirit that inhabits the Tiber River Tavern. According to what I was told, multiple people have looked into the windows while on the top floor of the tavern and to their surprise saw the face of a woman staring back at them. A woman named Jen also told me the same story. Imagine the feeling of looking into a reflective surface and seeing someone who isn't there staring back at you. I'd say that's pretty darn creepy!

I was also told that many bar patrons had reported seeing the apparition of a young woman in a flowing red dress walking down the stairs and heading toward the kitchen area of the tavern. According to another person that I spoke with, they had heard a story of a bright white figure going from one wall of the tavern to the other. The story may change in details a bit, but there is always one constant among the stories. That constant is that there is a spectral figure that roams the Tiber River Tavern.

Tommy went on to tell me about one major paranormal experience that he had at the Tiber River Tavern. According to Tommy, he was getting some ice to restock the bar one evening. He was standing at the top of a small staircase, when he watched as a small refrigerator moved. When hearing this story, I was thinking that the refrigerator door might have popped open or perhaps it had wheels and moved slightly. However Tommy elaborated on how the refrigerator was heavy and did not have wheels. Tommy told me that the refrigerator slid a foot away from the wall. Talk about poltergeist activity, that ghost must be on steroids! He also told me that the upstairs part of the tavern has always had a creepy feeling.

During my interviews with various people I came across some other interesting stories. Jen told me that she spoke to a former waiter at the Tiber River Tavern. The waiter told her that employees at the Tavern were not allowed to close the bar on their own. While this is generally good business policy for any establishment, it just seems that there may be a supernatural reason behind the rule as well.

The last story that I came across was from one of the workers in a restaurant in Ellicott City. According to this person, they had heard a story recently about a real estate broker who was showing the building off to a prospective buyer. This employee heard that during the tour, a loud crash was heard in the bar area. The real estate broker and prospective buyers went to investigate and found a broken wine glass on the floor. Even stranger was that the only glasses in the area were the water glasses hanging above the bar! I can only imagine the looks on the perspective buyers faces after hearing a loud crash and seeing that wine glass broken on the floor! While I can't confirm this story, it sure is a creepy tale.

So the next time that you are walking along Old Columbia Pike and see the old Tiber River Tavern, take a look in the windows. Be prepared for a surprise if you do however. You just might see the face of the Lady Spirit that inhabits the dwelling staring right back out at you.

UPDATE:

The building that housed the Tiber River Tavern now houses The Diamondback Bar and Restaurant. So make sure that you stop on in, get a bite to eat and ask the folks there about the building's resident ghosts!

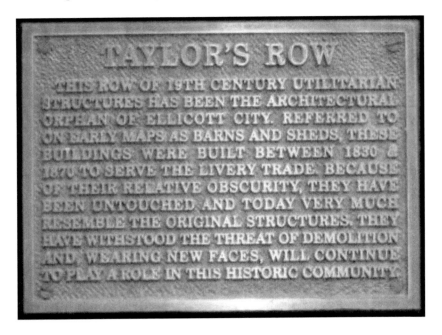

THE FORGET ME NOT FACTORY

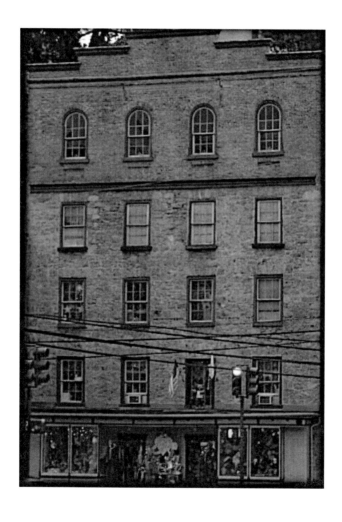

One of the gems of Main Street Ellicott City is The Forget Me Not Factory. The shop sells a cornucopia of items, from toys and collectibles to costuming for Halloween and renaissance era outfits. As a customer, I can get lost in this place for hours on end, looking at all the wondrous trinkets. The Christmas city and Halloween city displays alone are worth the trip to this shop of wonders. I personally enjoy seeing the zombie pirate on display, or dropping a coin in the automatic piano and hearing a tune. Whether you want to find a Christmas present for a loved one, or a Halloween decoration to spook the neighbors, The Forget Me Not Factory has something for you!

This place is truly built into the history of Ellicott City. You can literally touch the bedrock that the building is built into on the second floor of the store. It's quite a sight to see the various statues of gnomes along the rock face that serves as part of the wall for the building. It is ironic how this building is built into the very bedrock of the city, because the building itself has a history that goes back to the founding of the town.

The building that houses The Forget Me Not Factory has been around since the early 1800's. It has housed a bar, the Centre Lodge No. 40 and business offices in its early years. It held a newspaper and some early clothing manufacturing facilities. In the early 1900's it served as an early theater for silent films and has hosted dances.

During the warmer months, you can find Barry Gibson, Co-Owner of the building, outside of its doors entertaining young and old alike. He dazzles passers by on the street with his amazing bubble shows. It really isn't a trip to Ellicott City without seeing Barry aka "The Bubble Man" showing off his bubble making skills on Main Street outside of the store.

When Barry isn't amazing the tourists and locals with his bubble shows, he's telling some good stories about Ellicott City history and

[19]

folklore. If you ask any of the locals about the history and stories of the hauntings in Ellicott City, they will direct you to the Bubble Man. I had the opportunity to chat with the Bubble Man while conducting my research.

The first thing that Barry told me about was the time that he met a lady who actually worked in the building during the silent film era of the early 1920's. According to Barry, the woman played piano during the movies that were shown there. Back when people watched silent films, the films were just that...Silent. If you wanted a soundtrack for a film, you had someone play the soundtrack in the theatre. He also told me about the door on the top floor of the store. This door is now used for display purposes, but if you look beyond the display, you can see writing on this door. I was able to view this historic graffiti myself. I suggest going to take a look at the door when you visit this wonderful little store.

I asked Barry about the ghost stories involving The Forget Me Not Factory. Barry told me that they had some  "Ghost Busters" come into the store a few years ago. One of the investigators on that team was wearing a necklace with a cross on it. According to the story, the cross just fell off the necklace for no apparent reason. The way that it was described to me, there was a ring that kept the cross on the necklace. The ring was intact when it fell to the ground. Apparently they caught orbs on camera as well.

Since I am a paranormal investigator myself, I don't want you to get the impression that paranormal investigators are "Ghost Busters". I believe that it is likely that a team of paranormal investigators did an investigation at the store. It is unlikely that some people came into the store with proton packs ala Ghostbusters and tried to zap some ghosts. As for the Orb Phenomenon, there are many theories on these orbs. Whether or not they are ghostly phenomenon is up to you to decide. I personally do not believe that orbs are images of ghostly energy.

Barry also told me about a friend who visited the store one day. His friend was given a tour and allowed to see the theater portion of the shop. This friend stopped in the theatre and described seeing a woman being attacked by a man. The friend then walked over to a wall and said that a body was behind that wall. According to Barry, the wall was covering an old chimney for the place. Barry's friend claims to be psychic. One strange coincidence is that the incident with the cross falling off of the necklace occurred in the exact same spot as Barry's friend said the body was. No bodies have been recovered from that wall area to this day.

I also spoke with an employee of a shop that had no reported hauntings. This employee told me of an incident that she had experienced as a teen in The Forget Me Not Factory. According to her, she and a friend were taking a walk through the store, when the necklace that her friend was wearing just fell off of her neck. The clasp of the necklace was intact upon hitting the ground. This woman also told me that they experienced cold spots in the building. She also stated that she has a friend that works at the shop. This friend has told her that footsteps can be heard on the second floor when the place is empty. What's even more eerie is that though the sounds of footsteps can be heard, no one can be seen on the security camera on that floor.

Is The Forget Me Not Factory haunted? While I can't answer that question, I will say that there are far too many stories and tales among the town to dismiss the notion. I can't count how many people told me to visit The Forget Me Not Factory in my quest to find ghost stories about this town. If you visit this store, you will find every sort of creature, ranging from dragons to fairies. If you look hard enough and are lucky, you might even find yourself encountering a spirit from the past!

THE ANTIQUE DEPOT

Along Maryland Avenue sits a Mecca for those who seek antiques and classic collectibles. This little piece of antique heaven is called The Antique Depot. Whether you are looking for vintage toys and collectibles, classic military equipment or a really nice piece of antique furniture, this place has what you are looking for. Only one of the great antique shops in Ellicott City, The Antique Depot supports numerous vendors selling their diverse wares.

[24]

Located directly across the street from the B & O Railroad Museum, this property has been many things throughout the years. In the mid 1800's, it was the location of a store that sold lumber, lime and coal, all of which would have been shipped in or needed by the railroad. Later in that century, the warehouse was built and it became a Hardware and Farm Supply business. It remained that way until the late 1900's. Now the building houses The Antique Depot.

Though patrons come into the shop to find treasure from the past, they might end up with finding more than they bargained for and see a spirit from the past. According to Al, one of the vendors in the shop, the place has its fair share of paranormal activity. I had the opportunity to chat with Al and he had some amazing stories to tell about the store.

According to Al, there are a few spirits haunting The Antique Depot. He has even named one of them "Bart". Bart is a ghost that Al has seen on a number of occasions. Bart wears a round, Quaker type hat, with a black vest and a faded maroon shirt. Amazingly with this type of detailed description, Al has never once seen the Apparition's feet. Bart has appeared a few times for Al. One time, Al was behind the counter doing work, when he looked up to see Bart just standing there looking at him. This quite understandably scared Al. On occasion Bart can be seen sitting on a cart with luggage down one of the aisles as well. One minute you see the apparition and the next minute, it is gone. Al stated that when the ghost disappears from view, it looks like the effect that you see when you see heat coming off of a road.

There are 2 other spirits in the shop as well. According to Al, he and 2 other vendors/workers have seen the spirits of 2 little girls in the shop. The little girls appear to be wearing what has been described as nightgowns and have been seen on many occasions. Al even reports hearing the sounds of children's laughter and giggling on occasion. In one instance, Al recalled seeing both little girls standing in front of an old counter that he was standing behind.

The little girls aren't all giggling and laughs when he sees them though. Al described a feeling of distinct melancholy and sadness that overcomes you after seeing the little girls.

[26]

Yet another spirit inhabits The Antique Depot. Though Bart and the little girls are seen mainly on the first floor, the other spirit has been seen in the basement of the establishment. One day a vendor ventured into the basement and to her amazement saw a young woman. The young woman was dressed in the fashion of the late 1800's. Understandably the Vendor was frightened and bolted upstairs.

The spirits in this establishment aren't all looking to be seen either. According to Al, when you walk in the door on some mornings, there is an eerie feeling to the place. You get goose bumps and it feels as though there is electricity in the air. I was told about a meeting that Al was having with a lady who is now a former vendor. The spirits decided to make their presence known to this poor woman by giving her a chilly feeling. In the middle of the meeting the woman looked at Al with a look of fright and left the store. Soon after, she packed her wares and never returned to the shop.

So remember, when you go to The Antique Depot, keep an eye out for that perfect piece of treasure for your collection. Just keep in mind that there may be someone or something behind you wanting the same thing. There are definitely more things from the past than just the antiques in this shop!

TONGE ROW

Nestled along Old Columbia Pike lies a row of double homes made of stone. The site of these stone homes might strike one as odd, along that portion of the street that houses restaurants and other various businesses. But inside these homes you will find an array of small shops. These businesses peddle wares ranging from tattoos to jewelry and home accessories. This row of shops is usually the first thing that people see as they come to the town because one of the largest parking lots in

Ellicott City is found down the hill and behind the buildings. I always park in this lot because it lies right in the heart of town. The view of Tonge Row's shops from the parking lot is breathtaking and picturesque.

Tonge Row was built in the mid 1800's by the widow Ann Tonge (pronounced Tongue). According to some stories, the houses were a red-light district back then, though I have never been able to confirm that myself. Perhaps Mrs. Tonge just wanted to get into the real estate market of the mid 1800's. We will never know. Still the reason why Ann built the houses and what they were truly used for is a mystery that might never be solved.

Beyond Tonge Row's picturesque facade lies another mystery. This mystery involves many strange happenings reported by shop owners and customers alike. In researching this book, I discovered that most, if not all of the current shopkeepers don't like to talk about anything odd that happens in their stores. Luckily, I was once able to chat with the former owners of one of the stores along Tonge Row who were more than willing to regale me with stories of the unexplained things they and others had experienced. What they had to tell me was quite an amazing set of stories!

The first tale is of a female spirit that roams the shops of Tonge Row. This female spirit is called Cecilia. Like any young lady, Cecilia likes to talk and make her presence known. She apparently likes to walk up and speak into the ears of unsuspecting shoppers. Cecilia has reportedly even touched people. One such instance was when a painter was helping to remodel a room in one of the stores. This painter felt a tug on his clothing and then a ghostly whisper in his ear. I heard that the painter in question got that job done in record time. I sure would if it happened to me!

Cecilia doesn't just talk and touch people though. She also enjoys her toys. One story involves an evening break-in at one of the shops along Tonge Row. The next day the owners came in to find a broken window and the door ajar, but that wasn't the strangest part. Absolutely nothing was taken from the store. Stranger yet, a semi-circle of dolls and stuffed animals surrounded the door. Whether or not this was the ghost of Cecilia protecting the property, or just some young kids out to play a trick we will never know. However it is an interesting story. This wasn't the first story regarding moving dolls in a Tonge Row shop either!

Another story that I heard involved another incident when a room was being remodeled. A stuffed animal was flung across the room at an innocent worker one day while they were working alone. I can't imagine a greater fright than having a stuffed animal getting thrown at me when no one is around to do the throwing!

Dolls aren't the only things that move in the buildings. I have heard stories of a shop owner coming into their store in the morning to find that objects on a table have been flipped over! There was

even a story about a deck of cards being flung at one shop owner that inadvertently annoyed one of the spirits that inhabit the buildings!

Not all stories revolve around Miss Cecilia however. A former owner of a shop along Tonge Row told me that the ghosts like to make their presence known in other ways. This owner told me that while sitting downstairs in the shop, footsteps could be heard in the upper levels. Now this isn't strange in and of itself, however when the footsteps were heard, no one else was in the store. I was even told stories about how the owner would sit downstairs and see people moving throughout the store on the security monitor while no one else was in the store. Now that is some interesting viewing, it's just too bad that they didn't have a VCR hooked up to the screen when this happened!

Tonge Row is one of my favorite places to go. It is the first set of shops that I see when I get out of the car, and the last that I see when I'm leaving the city. I don't go to these great little shops just because of the ghost stories surrounding them. I go to these shops for the great things that they sell and the ambiance that they have. Though I have to admit that in the back of my mind, I always hope to have an encounter with one of the ghosts of Tonge Row!

JORDAN'S STEAKHOUSE

Now Portalli's

When you are looking for a really well made steak or a glass of fine wine, Jordan's Steakhouse is the place to go. Established on February 14th, 2002 Jordan's took its place among the fine dining establishments in the area. Jordan's is not the only fine dining establishment in Ellicott City, but it is the only place that offers you Valet Parking and Live Jazz. Jordan's is definitely one of Ellicott City's top restaurants if not one of Maryland's best!

The property that Jordan's Steakhouse currently occupies has been around since the mid to late 1800's. The property itself has housed everything from a personal dwelling, a grocery store, a barbershop and various restaurants and cafés. Before Jordan's existed, a restaurant called Main Street Blues occupied the property. Unfortunately a fire completely destroyed Main Street Blues in the 1990's. The property was rebuilt and Jordan's Steakhouse moved in.

During the day, Jordan's offers its customer's a great food, service and atmosphere. This fine dining establishment definitely gives its customers what they pay for! What customers don't get to witness is how the atmosphere changes when the restaurant closes its doors for the evening.

I was able to interview some of the workers and managers of the restaurant. These employees sure did have some stories to tell. The one story that sticks out in my mind is the creepy feeling that most of the people that I spoke to experience on the second floor of the restaurant. Specifically when you enter the dining area that has a piano inside, you get a chill like something is not right. The hair on the back of your neck stands up and you get goose bumps.

While I don't claim to be psychic, or have any sort of extra –sensory perception, I have experienced this creepy feeling first hand in that second floor room. I was allowed access to the room one Saturday afternoon while the restaurant was closed to take photographs for this book. I entered the room alone (big mistake if you're actually on an investigation) and had the same feeling overcome me that the workers described. Being the good Paranormal Investigator that I am, I pulled out my trusty digital voice recorder and placed it on a table near the piano. I then walked around the room and asked questions while snapping a few photographs for this book. This process took less than 2 minutes, and then I left the restaurant.

When I returned to my house, I did a quick review of the recording that I had recorded to see if I received any sort of response to my questions. While I didn't receive any sort of voice in response to my questions, I did hear a strange sound, much like a loud rumbling on the recording. As far as I could tell, there was nothing mechanical on at the time of the recording nor was there a natural source that could make the sound.

What I recorded was potentially Electronic Voice Phenomenon (EVP for short). For those that don't know what EVP is, let me explain. EVP is a voice (or sound) that shows up on an audio recording medium such as digital voice recorders. This voice or sound is one that was not present when recording the tape and is only heard upon playback. I contacted Jordan Naftal, Owner of Jordan's Steakhouse and was able to schedule an interview with him. From what I had heard from the employees at the restaurant, Jordan was the man to go to in order to hear some of the stories about the place. He didn't disappoint me with his tales of strange happenings at the restaurant.

Jordan has also encountered that strange feeling on the second floor. He told me that it just creeps him out. Jordan told me that while he has managers that close the restaurant now, he did the closing when first starting out. While closing, Jordan would be on the third floor, and get a strange sense that someone was at the bottom of the stairs. Strangely no one was in the restaurant with him at the time.

According to Jordan, he met someone who had lived in what would be the rear portion of the 2nd floor of the restaurant now about 40 years ago. Now I know what you are thinking, the person he met told him that there were many deaths in that humble dwelling. You would be wrong to think that, according to the person, nothing of that sort happened there.

After speaking with the person who lived at the property, Jordan thought that perhaps he was the only one having these experiences. He would soon discover that one of his Managers who had been closing the restaurant had an experience that might be a bit creepier than his own. According to Jordan, the gentleman in question is a fairly big guy (6 foot 5 inches). This gentleman told Jordan that he was closing the restaurant one evening when he heard the sound of footsteps going up the steps from the second floor to the third floor. Though a bit creeped out, Jordan was actually glad to hear that he wasn't alone in his experiences.

Jordan also told me about a story that he had heard in regards to the former owner of Main Street Blues. This story was not told to him directly, but he had heard of it and shared it with me. According to the story, the former owner of Main Street Blues had seen an apparition on the first floor of the restaurant one day. The apparition was that of a man wearing an outfit described as that of an undertaker.

After the interview, I pulled out the voice recorder that I had used during my previous visit. I explained to Jordan when and where I had used the recorder. We reviewed the audio recording and listened to the strange sound that was captured. Being two logical men, we tried to figure out a reasonable explanation for the sound. Jordan offered that just below the place where I recorded the audio, a kitchen stove exhaust fan exists. I stated that I didn't hear anything like that kick on during my audio recording. Jordan told me that he didn't believe that anyone would have needed to turn on the fan at the time of the recording. We both agreed that the sound heard on the audio recording was interesting, but needed further review.

I can't tell you for certain that Jordan's Steakhouse is haunted. There are many stories and strange experiences that have been reported by the employees, management and the owners. Even I had an experience at Jordan's that I can't explain. Was it a ghost from the past? I can't be certain. What I can be certain of is that this fine dining establishment seems to offer an observant person more than just a good dining experience. If one day you find yourself seated on the second floor enjoying the dining experience at Jordan's and you feel a strange feeling, don't think that you are going crazy. Others have felt the same feeling that you are experiencing.

UPDATE:

Recently Jordan's closed its doors. There is a new restaurant at the location called Portalli's. I stopped in the restaurant to say hi and the staff was very friendly. So don't be afraid to come on down to Portalli's for a great meal, and if you're lucky, one of the staff might tell you a story about the ghosts that reportedly haunt the restaurant!

BEAN HOLLOW

Nothing says historic, small town like the local coffee houses. While strolling along the south side of Main Street, you might catch a waft of the coffee brewing inside this little coffee shop. If you suddenly feel an urge to go inside, don't fight it. Inside this café, you will find a wide variety of coffee and tea concoctions to soothe your pallet. There is also a nice selection of deserts and other various sweets to satisfy that sweet tooth of yours. Inside you will find a very relaxing atmosphere with walls adorned with decorations from the past. There is even an old coffee-roasting machine from the turn of the century sitting inside the dining area. So sit back and enjoy the company of your friends while sipping on the beverage of your choice.

You would never believe what this fine little coffee house was in the past by looking at the inside. Look on the outside however and you will see a stone arch with the word "Easton" on it. This property was once owned by the Easton Family.

The building itself was once a Funeral Home built in the 1930's. Though the building itself is fairly new, the actual property housed an undertaking business since the late 1800's. The Easton Funeral Home stayed in business until the mid 20th century.

While researching this book, I was able to chat with a few of the employees of the Bean Hollow. They sure did have some strange stories to tell me about this humble little coffee shop! It seems that the ghosts like to be playful and a lot of times enjoy helping the staff out with their work.

One employee told me about one evening that she needed to mop the floor of the café. She had gathered all of the supplies to mop the floor and was about to start, when she realized that she had forgotten to do something in another room. She went to that room and left the mop and bucket alone in the café. This employee returned five minutes later to find that the entire floor had been mopped. She told me that no one else could have mopped the floor because the only other employee in the place was off doing work in another part of the building. I guess that the ghost just wanted to do its fair share of the housekeeping!

Another strange tale regarding this helpful ghost came from Meg, Manager of the Bean Hollow. One fateful morning, she came to open the restaurant. Too her understandable surprise, she found that all of the coffee had been brewed. After hearing this story, I think that the resident phantom should be put on the payroll. After all good help is hard to find and this spirit seems to enjoy the work!

Apparently this spirit does need to unwind and relax once in a while. This ghost's hobbies seem to include opening locked doors. Employees of the café will go down to the basement to get various items. When they leave the basement, the door is then locked. After the employees return to the basement door to get another item, they find that the door has been unlocked and opened. I'd say that's pretty darn strange. Of course the ghost may just be trying to be helpful by opening the door for its fellow coworkers.

So the question on my mind is whether the Bean Hollow is haunted or not? It's one that I can't answer for you. However I suggest that the next time you are in the café, drinking your favorite cup of coffee or tea, strike up a conversation with one of the employees about their ghost. And just remember that should you happen to get up from your table to use the rest room and return to a freshly cleaned table, or mopped floor, that one of the ghostly residents of the coffee house might have done the job instead of the more corporeal employees.

Ghosts of Ellicott City by Russ Noratel

THE WAGON WHEEL

This small store is located in Tiber Alley and lays just a hop, skip and a jump from the Bean Hollow. In the course of my research I discovered that this small building was once owned by the Easton Family. The building was used as a horse stable and equipment storage for the funeral home. As you can probably imagine, equipment storage means that they stored caskets at the location.

The Wagon Wheel now resides in this building. The Wagon Wheel is a little antique shop that sells all kinds of delightful treasures from the past. One of the treasures still stored at the Wagon Wheel has been there for at least ninety years. This treasure is most certainly not for sale. This treasure is a horse drawn hearse that was used for funerals.

Now with a used hearse sitting on the top floor of the shop, some would believe the place to be haunted. According to the owner, there is a very popular story revolving around the hearse. From his recollection of the story, the hearse

actually moves on its own.

Hearing a story like this, I had to investigate for myself. I went over to look at the hearse. While you can clearly see the hearse, it would be fairly impossible for it to move, as it's boxed in by various pieces of merchandise. The owner himself said that he has never seen the hearse move.

The only story that the Owner told me about his shop came from when he first moved into the building. The owner would hear the floors creaking. Though he came to the logical conclusion that the building was old and old boards will creak. Perhaps the story of the moving hearse came from this owner's recollection of hearing some boards creaking one evening and passing the story on to a customer. We will never know.

While you may not find any ghosts at the Wagon Wheel, you will be able to see a piece of history just sitting on the second floor. Of course at this store, each piece of merchandise is a piece of history and a treasure unto itself. If you find yourself walking down Tiber Alley one day and see the Wagon Wheel open, stop in and check out all of the little treasures from the past that are within its walls. Perhaps you may even wish to take one home with you.

B&O RAILROAD MUSEUM: ELLICOTT CITY STATION

One of the first buildings that you see upon entering Ellicott City is the B&O Railroad Museum. Railroad enthusiasts from all around come to visit this historic landmark. The Museum offers visitors a glimpse into Ellicott City's past with various displays and artifacts to view. There is even a beautiful model train display showing the path of the railroad through Ellicott City and the surrounding area. Historians and re-enactors can be found at the station on the weekends showing the clothing of a time long past and giving a unique view of life in the nineteenth century.

The B&O Railroad Museum sits upon land that was gifted to the railroad by the Ellicott Brothers in the early 1800's with the stipulation that a depot be built at the location. By 1831 the Railroad Station building was completed. The building was constructed of granite, which came from local quarries. This train station played a pivotal role in the Battle of Monacacy, receiving the dead and wounded from the battle. Originally the station was equipped to service steam engines, but eventually the engines themselves outgrew the building and the engines had to be serviced in the Baltimore train yards.

The station was used for passenger service until the 1950's. Freight was shipped through the station until the 1970's. Now the building houses the B&O Railroad Museum: Ellicott City Station, which has become one of the staple attractions of the town.

Through my research into this historic structure, I was able to find a few stories that suggest that some travelers never actually left the train station. While I've never had a paranormal experience at the museum, I have been with friends who had a weird experience. My friend, her husband and I decided to take a trek into Ellicott City one day and decided to visit the Railroad Museum. Inside we found a few re-enactors manning their posts. After exploring the Train Station building, we decided to go out to the platform area. My friend went outside through the door and noticed something strange dart

past her field of vision. She described to me a small shadowy figure that darted down the path and hid behind a barrel that was sitting there. I remember seeing the startled look that she gave me after the incident that told me that she had definitely seen something that was out of the ordinary!

While speaking to one local bartender in a nearby restaurant, I was told an amazing story regarding the train station. According to the bartender, a dishwasher from his restaurant was walking to work one foggy morning when he passed the Train Station. At the station was a little boy standing all alone. The boy approached the dishwasher and asked him for help finding his mommy. Being a Good Samaritan, the dishwasher agreed to help the boy, not giving much thought as to why the boy was wearing clothing from a bygone era. The dishwasher took the boy by the hand and the two walked the short distance to the restaurant. When the pair approached the restaurant, the boy let go of the dishwasher's hand. The dishwasher turned toward where the boy was standing and saw nothing but the wisps of morning fog.

Another story that I unearthed in regards to the B&O Railroad Museum comes from the book Ghost Encounters, Tales of the Supernatural Residents of Historic Ellicott City by Mollie Back and Brian Wolle. According to this story, a re-enactor had stayed the night at the Railroad Museum. This young man was having trouble sleeping and decided to slip outside to take in the night air. It was a dark, foggy night when along came a man who was walking his old dog.

The two chatted for a while regarding the history of the railroad during the civil war. One particular story discussed was about a soldier

who was shot while walking picket duty one fateful night. The soldier soon died of his wounds. This soldier had befriended a dog that was always by his side, even when walking the picket line. The dog stopped eating and died soon after his soldier companion's tragic death.

Well the conversation ended and the man and his dog walked off. While they were walking off, the man's clothing changed to that of a civil war soldier and the dog seemed to become more youthful and energetic. An eerie voice came out of the fog. The voice said that the pair had done their duty and walked the picket line ever since, guarding the Rail station.

Whether you are a train enthusiast, or an avid historian, the B&O Railroad Museum has something to offer you. While walking through the halls of the station you are sure to take in all the history and enjoy yourself. Just remember that many people have been to this place, and some may have never left. Most importantly, if you are walking past the station on a foggy night and see someone dressed in nineteenth century clothing, that might not be a re-enactor that you are looking at, it might just be one of the phantom residents of Ellicott City!

Ghosts of Ellicott City by Russ Noratel

THE PATAPSCO FEMALE INSTITUTE

Should you wish to take an uphill trek to take a look into the past, The Patapsco Female Institute is the place that you want to go. What once awaited onlookers was a large building designed in the Greek revival style. A large stone staircase with large pillars greeted its visitors. The building itself was made from the granite quarried from the local area. Now all that remains is a ruined shell of what was once a great building.

The Patapsco Female Institute opened in 1837, offering young ladies of the time a unique educational opportunity. Things didn't go too well initially for the school until Almira Hart Lincoln Phelps came along in 1841 and signed on to lead the school. Mrs. Phelps was the superstar of her time in the field of education. To put it in perspective, Having Almira Hart Lincoln Phelps sign on to lead the school, would be like having Cal Ripkin Jr. sign on to coach your little league team.

Many students from the south were enrolled at the school. Some students came from Canada and some students were Native American. The school prospered under the gentle guidance of Mrs. Phelps for many years. After the death of her husband, Mrs. Phelps left the school in 1856. The school itself closed in 1891.

Since the school closed in 1891, the building has served many different functions. For a time the building served as a hotel and a theatre. The building also was a convalescent home during World War 1 and World War 2. The building itself was eventually abandoned in the mid 20th, century. In the 1960's, Howard County purchased the property, and the

Friends of the Patapsco Female Institute was formed. The building fell into extreme disrepair and ruin over the next couple of decades. Vandals sprayed graffiti and did quite a bit of damage to the ruins in that time. In 1987, first phase of the stabilization project began. They used the original granite that the building was made from to do so. By 1995 the stabilization project was completed. A great deal of excavation of the site has also occurred, unearthing over 30000 artifacts from the past.

Among the ruins, there is also another story to be told. This story is that of poor Annie. Annie was a student at the school in the era of Mrs. Phelps. Her stay at the school was not one of joy or happiness, but one of misery and sorrow. Little Annie desperately wanted to be released from the school to return home, but her family would have nothing of that. Unfortunately for Annie, she was eventually allowed a release, but it was the release of death. Poor Annie contracted pneumonia in her first year at the school and died.

It is said that Annie's spirit never left the building that she so desperately wanted to leave in life. According to Ghost Encounters, Tales of the Supernatural Residents of Historic Ellicott City, by Mollie Back and Brian Wolle, the spirit of a young girl in a flowing white dress can be seen walking through the ruins. The spirit is seen crossing from one solid stone wall and entering into a solid stone wall on the other side of the room. According to the book, visitors visiting the ruin swear that they feel the presence of someone behind them, only to turn around to find no one there. There are even reports of people having strange experiences with cold breezes passing by them or cold areas settling around them.

Another story of Annie comes from Troy Taylor. In this accounting, a visitor to the ruins of Patapsco Female Institute was separated from their group. To this visitor's surprise, the spectral form of a girl in a white dress appeared on the porch at the top of the steps. The apparition walked down the steps and onto the lawn, then promptly vanished before the visitor's eyes! Holy full-bodied apparition Batman!

I had the opportunity to speak with a person that had some interesting stories to tell me about what visitors to the Patapsco Female Institute had reported. One such report regarded an apparition of a girl in a white dress being seen on the porch at the top of the staircase. This report seems to follow along the lines as those stories told by Back, Wolle and Taylor.

There have been reports of lights being seen by visitors. An eerie blue light can be seen moving in the upstairs windows of the ruins. Stranger yet, there are not any floors on that level of the structure.

There was even one story in which a light was seen emanating up through the now non-existent roof of the structure.   There have also been reports about music being heard coming from the ruins. The music doesn't seem to have an explainable origin.

You can find everything from children's camps and archeological digs to plays and tours being held at the Patapsco Female Institute during the summer. You can even book your wedding at the site. Whether or not The Patapsco Female Institute is haunted is up to you to decide.   Keep in mind that most of the stories revolve around the phantom schoolgirl Annie, but there is no telling how many people have died at this location during it's time as a convalescent home. In the event you wish to visit the site or take a tour, go to the Mount Ida Visitor's center and ask about their tours. Just remember to keep up with the group during your tour. If you don't, you might have a ghostly experience at this historic site!

MOUNT IDA

Sitting at the bottom of the slope near the Patapsco Female Institute is this majestic mansion. As you pull up along Sarah's Lane, you see the tall, white, square columns of the old porch where it is obvious that the porch once stood. Looking at this Mansion from the outside, you can imagine how the home once looked in its day.

Mount Ida was originally built for William Ellicott, the grandson of one of Ellicott City's founders, Andrew Ellicott, around 1830. Unfortunately for William, he would not enjoy his home for long, because he died in the late 1830's. The house itself would be the last built in Ellicott City proper by a member of the Ellicott Family.

The next family to take up residence at Mount Ida was the Tyson Family. Purchased by Judge John S. Tyson, he and his family lived in the mansion for many years. After Judge Tyson and his wife died, their only son, John, inherited the property. Unfortunately, John died in a horrible boating accident. His three sisters resided at the residence until the last surviving sister, Miss Ida Tyson died in the 1920's.

The last family to reside in the mansion was the Clark Family. They lived there until the 1960's.

Now the Friends of

the Patapsco Female Institute are headquartered in the building. The only place accessible to the public is the first floor. The building has been modified into a museum to display historical artifacts unearthed from archeological digs at the Patapsco Female Institute. You can find everything from drawings of the Patapsco Female Institute and original diplomas, to pieces of broken pottery and wood from the original structure of the school. You can find at least one room which has been made to look like it could be lived in. That room really gives you the feeling of how Mount Ida could be a home to someone. Located in the basement according to one of the workers is a lab dedicated to the unearthed artifacts from the archeological digs of the Patapsco Female Institute. The basement lab and the third floor are off limits to the public. One thing that is offered for those looking to take the tour of the school is a video, which gives information about the Patapsco Female Institute and Mount Ida's history. I strongly suggest viewing this video if you are interested in the history of either structure.

While Mount Ida is steeped in history, it usually takes second place to the Patapsco Female

Institute when it comes to stories of the paranormal. However there are stories related to Mount Ida. Most every person that I spoke to in the course of my research for this book directed me first to the Patapsco Female Institute, and then to Mount Ida when it came to looking for haunted places in Ellicott City. While many people knew some sort of story regarding the school, none could give me a clear story as to why they thought Mount Ida was haunted.

Luckily I knew of one story that Troy Taylor had spoken about on his website entry about Mount Ida. According to Taylor's story, Miss Ida, the last survivor of the Tyson family to live in the mansion, had a thing for carrying around a large key ring. This key ring would jingle as all key rings do. It seems that quite a few people have reported hearing the sounds of keys jingling, like those on a key ring that someone is carrying.

I wasn't able to find any other stories besides the one told by Taylor. However I did ask some of the employees about the suspected haunting of Mount Ida. Most of the employees I asked, would not comment on the ghost tales. I was able to find one employee that spoke on the condition of anonymity and stated that Mount Ida is haunted.

Of all the reported hauntings in Ellicott City, I believe that this ghost may perhaps be the friendliest. Of all that I have read and heard about Miss Ida, she was a kind woman in life. I can't imagine that she would be any less kind in death. She loved the house that she lived in. Even in death, she must want to watch over the place that she so loved in her life.

You may not find the people at Mount Ida willing to tell you a story about ghosts. But you will find them more than willing to tell you all about the rich history of both the Mansion and the Patapsco Female Institute. The people who work at Mount Ida are very friendly and extremely knowledgeable of the history of Ellicott City as well as the school and Mount Ida. You can ask them pretty much any question about those subjects and they'll have an answer.

So the next time you are looking to take a tour of the Patapsco Female Institute, make sure that you keep enough time to take a look around the Mount

Ida mansion, before rushing up to the school ruins. In your time there, be sure to keep your ears open, because you will find some really interesting historical information. Just remember that if you listen hard enough, you might just hear the sounds of Miss Ida's keys jingling behind you!

THE JUDGE'S BENCH

Like any small town, there are a few local watering holes where everyone knows your name. One of the most well known pubs in Ellicott City is The Judge's Bench. Anyone (21 and over please) who visits Ellicott City should stop in and try one of the various brews that they have for sale. While having a drink, sit back in one of the nice leather chairs on the second floor while watching the game on the television. Or you can play a game of darts or foosball with your friends. Of course you can always sit at the bar and watch the big screen while drinking a beer with the local patrons.

The building itself has been around since the mid to late 1800's. It has served as a grocery store and a flooring store. The most recent incarnation of the building has been the pub, which has been around for a while. Actually the bar itself had a recent change of ownership and is currently run by

Mike and Jane Johnson.

While you will find a good time and a great, relaxed atmosphere at The Judge's Bench, there is also a much darker side to the pub. Many years ago a young girl named Mary committed suicide on the third floor of the building. It is said that even though her physical form ceased to exist, her spiritual presence never left the building.

It is fact that Mary committed suicide; there are varying stories as to why she did so. One of those stories is that of unrequited love for a man. Mary loved this man and he never returned that love. The anguished Mary then hung herself in a fit despair. The other story was that Mary and a dashing young man were head over heels in love with each other. Mary's parents did not like the young man and forbade Mary from seeing him. The heartsick Mary was so upset by her parent's decision, that she ended her own life. Perhaps Mary believed that she would meet with her beau in the afterlife.

I was able to interview quite a few people in the course of my research of The Judge's Bench. One of them was my friend, Vince Wilson, who had conducted numerous investigations of the old pub. There were also numerous patrons willing to tell me some of the strange stories related to the establishment.

[75]

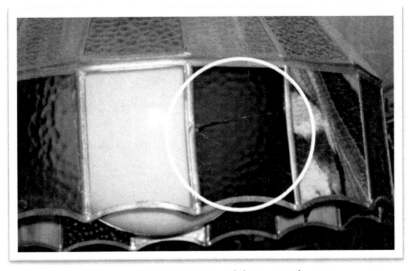

One story that I was told was about a patron named Shorty who had been coming to the bar for decades. Unfortunately for this Shorty, he was diagnosed with liver damage by his doctor and told not to drink another drop of alcohol. Shorty accepted that he would have to stop drinking, but still wanted to say goodbye to his friends at the bar. So Shorty came into the bar, sat at his normal barstool at the corner of the bar and ordered a Ginger Ale.

He then made the announcement to his friends that he would not be coming back to the bar on account of his health. At the moment he made his announcement, the lamp hanging above the bar where he was sitting crashed down upon the bar!

Understandably this startled both Shorty and everyone else in the bar. Everyone agreed that Mary must have been upset by Shorty's announcement. The actual lamp that fell was pointed out to me. The stained glass lampshade actually has one pane, which is cracked!

Another story that I heard was during the time was of a previous owner. This owner was named Buzzy. Good ole Buzzy came in one day to get the bar ready for business that night. To his surprise, he looked behind the bar only to find that many of the liquor bottles were missing. He looked down on the floor behind the bar and saw the bottles lying on their sides in a straight line! This was definitely strange since he had definitely not done this himself before closing the night before. It seems that Mary wanted a change of scenery that evening.

The bathrooms on the first floor bar also seem to have activity as well. At least one bartender has been closing the bar and heard the faucets in the bathroom come on by themselves. Another former employee has claimed to have an experience with the downstairs bathroom. This worker was vacuuming one day when a faint sound was coming from the bathroom. The worker turned off the vacuum and could hear the sound of toilet paper unraveling in the restroom. Needless to say, this surprised the poor employee because no one else was in the bar at the time. Being the curious sort, this worker went to investigate and found that the entire roll of toilet paper was unraveled on the floor. While investigating the unraveling toilet paper, the vacuum cleaner suddenly turned back on all by itself!

I found out about one of the most recent incidents while interviewing Jane Johnson, Co-Owner of the Judge's Bench. According to Mrs. Johnson, she was renovating the attic about 6 months after they had purchased the Judge's Bench. Mind you this story takes place in the area where Mary hung herself so many years ago. Mrs. Johnson told me that she was alone in the building, doing some renovations of the attic. Seemingly out of nowhere, Mrs. Johnson felt a cold breeze go across her arm. Being the logical person that she is, Mrs. Johnson looked around for any possible source of the cold breeze and could not find one. Mrs. Johnson told me that she occasionally talks to Mary, just to keep her spirit happy and to let Mary know that she hasn't been forgotten. As a side note, Vince Wilson told me that during one of his last investigations at the Judge's Bench, there were some weird EMF readings taken in the attic area of the bar.

While I can't say that The Judge's Bench is haunted, I can say that there are too many great stories to deny the possibility. I can say that if you visit this local pub, you will find a relaxing and friendly atmosphere with great service and hospitality. Should you find yourself sitting at the bar and the lamp on the corner begins to move, or if you go into the bathroom to find the faucet running, say hi to Mary; she is just letting you know that she is still around!

ELLICOTT MILLS BREWERY

Ellicott Mills Brewery is one of the best little Bar/Restaurants along Main street. They have a wide variety of beer to choose from, including foreign, domestic and their very own specialty brews. The food at this restaurant is top quality and very reasonably priced. Personally I really enjoy the crab-cake sandwiches and burgers. At any time of the day you will find a relaxed atmosphere and a friendly wait staff ready to take your order.

The granite building that the Ellicott Mills Brewery currently resides in was built in the late 1800's by the Talbot family. The Talbot's were in the lumber and building supply business. This building housed the Talbot Hardware store for many years. During the course of my research, I actually came across someone that remembered the old Talbot Hardware store on the property.

I really enjoyed researching the ghost stories involving this restaurant because was able to do so while enjoying my meal on the second floor of the restaurant. Over the course of my meal I asked my waiter if he had heard any ghost stories in relation to the restaurant. He sure had a tale to tell.

[81]

According to my waiter, a man had hung himself in the corner of the upstairs portion of the restaurant back in the 1920's around the time of the stock market crash. Back then, the upstairs area was office space. The way that I understood the story, the man was spotted in Tiber Park acting very strangely. Well, the reports of the man's strange antics caused someone to look in on his office. What they found was his body hanging there. Stranger yet was that his body seemed to have been there for a

few days, including those days he was seen acting strangely in Tiber Park. I was not able to confirm that a man had hung himself in the building during the course of my research. The waiter told me that the area where the man had hung himself was called "The Coffin". It was even pointed out to me how the area does seem to resemble a coffin because of how it is situated between the stairs and the window. The waiter told me that I should speak to some of the other employee's in the restaurant and hear some of their interesting stories. I took his advice and was amazed at the stories that I was told.

I journeyed downstairs and met Carey, the bartender. Carey has had some experiences with the upstairs of the restaurant. One evening the women's bathroom on the first floor was not available for use. Carey found herself using the second floor bathroom. She  made 4 trips to the second floor restroom that night. I must note that according to her story, the second floor was closed for the evening. For the first 3 trips, the second floor was dark and quiet. On the 4th, trip Carey noticed a flickering in the corner. That flickering was coming from a candle, which had apparently ignited on its own volition. Carey told me that this is not an isolated incident either. Other employees have reported the same thing happening on occasion. I was also told that during the evening and morning when the upstairs is closed, you feel a creepy feeling when going up there.

Speaking of stories involving the upstairs, I was told a story about a manager at the restaurant that was closing one morning. At around 3 am, this manager heard footsteps on the second floor. This surprised the manager because no one else was in the place! The footsteps started coming down the stairs at what sounded like a running pace. At this point the manager expected to see someone coming down the stairs toward him, but no one was there. That manager closed the restaurant at a lightning pace that night, that's for sure! This isn't the only case of movement being heard on the second floor when no one is supposed to be up there. I have also heard that other employees will occasionally hear the sound of moving furniture on the second floor, when that floor is closed!

The candle story wasn't the only one that Carey relayed to me. Apparently the spirit who haunts the restaurant enjoys mimicking people's voices and calling out names of the employees. One evening Carey was working in the bar, when she heard her fiancé call her name. Now this in and of itself is not unusual because her fiancé works at the

restaurant. However on this evening, her fiancé was at home watching their baby!

There have been reports of activity on the first floor of the restaurant. The activity in question occurred in the kitchen. According to Joaquin, the Kitchen Manager a pot flew off the shelf in the kitchen and landed 5 feet away. I asked him to show me the area and he not only showed me the shelf, but the very pot that had flown off the shelf! From what I saw, there was no logical explanation for why a pot would be able to move from that point on the shelf to sitting upright on the floor 5 feet away.

At the Ellicott Mills Brewery, you will definitely find a wide variety of spirits. Most of these spirits are of the alcoholic variety though. However if the stories that I was relayed are true, you might just encounter more than you bargained for in this great dining establishment. If for some reason you hear your name being called by someone who couldn't possibly be there, or you see a candle, light up in front of you, don't fret, it's just the resident spirit of the Ellicott Mills Brewery making sure that you know it's there!

WESSELS
FLORIST

In my humble opinion every little town needs its own flower shop and Ellicott City is no different. People come to a flower shop for all different types of occasions. Whether it is a sorrowful occasion such as a loved one in a hospital or a young man trying to court his beautiful lady love, people need a place to get their flower arrangements for every type of occasion.

The building that Wessell's Florist currently occupies wasn't always there. Originally there was a tin shop and stable on the property. The old buildings were torn down when the Patapsco Bank purchased the property in 1903. By 1905 the current building was erected for use by the Patapsco Bank. The building itself is constructed in such a way that invokes a feeling that the bank is stable and that you can trust the company. By the 1980's the bank became the First National Bank just before closing its doors forever.

There have been a number of businesses that have taken up residence in the building over the years. These businesses include a café, craft store and even a stamp shop. The Su Casa furniture store was the most recent resident until Wessell's Florist moved in.

The stories of paranormal activity don't begin with those told to me by a Wessell's employee though. Apparently the folks who worked at Su Casa had some run-ins with the paranormal. I was able to speak with an employee at Su Casa, which is currently located at 8037 Frederick Road. According to him there were a few stories regarding the store when it was located in the bank building. Unfortunately he couldn't remember most of them. He was able to relay one story to me regarding an employee that had closed the store one evening.

The story goes that there were a few beds on display in the store. Well this employee went about making the beds. The employee then locked the store for the night and went home. The unfortunate employee had to help open the store the very next day. To their surprise, they opened the store to find that all the beds had been messed up over the evening. Suffice to say, I was disappointed to hear that my source couldn't remember any more stories about the old store location.

Being that I'm the curious type I had to go down to Wessell's and at least try to interview some of the employees. I will admit that I had been told by a few people that the folks at Wessell's weren't fans of ghost stories. However I was pleasantly surprised when I entered the store and found a wonderful manager named Stephanie who was more than willing to chat with me.

According to Stephanie the folks that work in the store enjoy their music. They listen to it on an old style CD Radio. She told me that on a few occasions that radio will just come on all by itself. If that isn't strange enough, a pattern seemed to emerge from the story that I had heard from the Su Casa employee. Apparently this radio is turned off at night at closing time. When employees come in the next day it is playing music. I was allowed to examine the radio, because I believed that a remote control might be able to turn the radio on and off. From what I saw, there was no remote control for the radio; it seemed to be a manually controlled. So it seems to be a spirit that enjoys music in Wessell's Florist.

Another story regarded a former employee at Wessell's Florist. Apparently this employee was standing on the first floor one day when she looked over and saw a small child running up the stairs to the second floor. Being that the employee was fairly certain that a child had not entered the store this surprised the poor woman. She searched the store high and low only to find that no child was in the store.

Whether or not Wessell's Florist is haunted is not for me to decide. All I can tell you is that when you go there, you will see and smell wonderful things as you enter the establishment. If you look carefully, you will see the remnants of the old bank within the building. Stephanie was kind enough to let me view the historic bank vault door. If you think you want to visit Wessell's Florist looking for a great flower arrangement and hear the radio playing in the background, you might recall that there may be a spectral customer listening to the songs as well.

COCOA LANE

If you wish to define a small town, just take a look

at its bars and restaurants. More is better in this case. You can find many great food establishments and bars throughout Ellicott City. Cacao Lane combines both bar and restaurant all in one. The restaurant furniture gives you a classic sense of how things were in the olden days. Heck you can even find an antique cash register right behind the bar. The sight of that cash register was both a shock and a pleasure to

[93]

see while I was doing my research.

The three and a half story structure that Cacao Lane currently resides in was built in the 1830's. Like many buildings in Ellicott City, the building is constructed from cut stone from local quarries. The building really stands out to an onlooker because of its grey appearance with the giant green awning displaying the name Cocoa Lane proudly on the first floor.

There have been many businesses in this building over the years. Some of them have included a millinery, grocery, bar, pool hall and taxi-cab company. When Hurricane Agnes flooded the town the first floors of the building were filled with mud and debris. In 1974, Cacao Lane opened its doors to the public.

With such a rich history, there is no wonder that stories of ghostly phenomenon circulate about Cacao Lane. I had the pleasure of interviewing a couple of people at Cacao Lane. The first of which was a gentleman named Ed who was tending bar at the time of my visit.

Ed regaled began by telling me about an old cook at the restaurant named George that had worked at the restaurant until his death from cancer. In remembrance of George's hard work, his name was kept on the schedule even after his tragic death. One day an employee was in the kitchen and started kidding around about why George hadn't been taken off the schedule so long after his death. Suddenly the pots and pans started moving on their own and banging together in the kitchen. I guess that George didn't like some new employee telling him that he shouldn't be on the schedule!

There was another story regarding the first floor. According to Ed, one evening when the restaurant was closing a strange thing happened on the first floor. Apparently, a mirror on the wall behind the bar lifted up and moved on its own. At the same time the phones and intercoms began making weird noises. The mirror didn't crash to the ground however, it just moved. It seems that the resident ghost just wanted to make its presence known, not cause 7-years bad luck. Ed wasn't the only one to tell this story, I was also told the same thing by a waitress.

Later in the same day I was able to speak to a longtime employee at Cacao Lane named Jamal. I must say that he came highly recommended by his fellow employees in regards to knowing the paranormal happenings in the restaurant. I found that everyone was right; Jamal did have some interesting tales to tell.

It seems that Jamal has had a few close encounters of the spooky kind while on the job. The first tale that Jamal told me occurred while he was speaking with a patron sitting at the bar. Out of the corner of Jamal's eye he noted a human shaped figure wearing a white shirt walk through the hallway near the restroom. This occurred at least twice in 20 minutes time. Of course I asked if it could have been a customer or employee, and Jamal was certain that it wasn't.

The second tale that Jamal told me about was an incident that occurred while he was waiting on a dining table directly in front of the first floor bar. Jamal told me that before he had gone to wait on the table, all bar stools were facing the bar. However when he turned around from waiting on the

[96]

customers, one of those barstools was completely turned around facing toward the dining table. This of course surprised Jamal considering that he had only had the barstools out of his sight for a few moments time.

I was also told about a strange incident that took place in a restroom. Jamal stated that one of the employees had gone to the restroom and after washing his hands like any good restaurant worker turned to leave and the faucet came back on. Jamal didn't say how the employee reacted, but I sure would be a bit disturbed by that occurrence.

Since it sounded like most of the activity had surrounded the first floor I asked Jamal if anything occurred on the second floor. Jamal told me that when they lock up the upstairs portion of the restaurant, he feels like someone is always watching him. I was told the same story by Ed as well. Yours truly was invited to come back late that night to help close up the upstairs so I could experience the feeling, however I didn't have the time to do so. I had to settle for taking a few digital photos of the upstairs while it was empty for this book during the day instead. Though I didn't capture any anomalies on my photos, I did feel like something wasn't right while standing in that empty room.

Speaking of the upstairs portion of Cacao Lane, there have been other strange activities reported. Jamal told me that one evening some employees heard the distinct sounds of footsteps coming down the steps from the uppermost level. These two employees didn't want to know who or what was coming down the steps, since they knew that no one was in that part of the building to come down the steps, so they ran!

I highly recommend visiting Cacao Lane. The wait staff and bartenders are very friendly. You can order anything from a Burger and fries to Rack of Lamb. Of course while you are eating, if you happen to catch site of someone moving next to you, don't worry, it's probably just one of the spectral patrons of Cacao Lane, there to enjoy the restaurant.

OLD SARAH AND DESMONDS

My first memory of coming to Ellicott City involved this great little café nestled inside of what appeared to be an old row home which appealed to a younger version of me. I entered this great little café and was struck by the aroma various coffee's and pastries. My eyes were delighted at the simple set up of the multi level coffee house. The atmosphere at the place was so great that I remember taking a few dates there to spend an evening chatting over coffee. Of course things change over the years, and Ellicott City is known just for that. Sarah and

Desmond's Gourmet Bakery now resides along Old Columbia Pike.

The location where the Old Sarah and Desmond's had set up shop was constructed in the early 1800's. The building is actually one of the oldest in the northern part of Main Street Ellicott City. Like most buildings in the town, the 3 and a half story building is constructed from local granite. Originally the building was just a run of the mill (pardon the mill town pun) residence. There have been various other businesses at the location. The building has housed a confectionary and athletic club. In more recent history the building has housed multiple coffee houses, including Sarah and Desmond's, a wine shop, and back in the 1990's Nature's Tapestries was at the location. Currently the building has been renovated and is now just waiting for its next business to set up shop.

As you know, I take great joy in tracking down sources to tell me stories of paranormal activity that occurs in the town. This time was no different. I walked into the new location for Sarah and Desmond's Gourmet Bakery and was reminded of their time at the old coffee house by the smells and sounds. On this day I had the opportunity to speak with the owner of the establishment, Desmond.

Originally I asked Desmond if there had been any paranormal activity reported at the shop's current location and he told me that there wasn't anything to report. To my delight, he did have some interesting stories regarding the shop's old location along Main Street.

Desmond told me that whatever is at the old shop likes to watch people. The story goes that when someone was in the second floor kitchen, they would feel as though someone was watching them. It was described as the feeling one has when a person is standing behind them. Desmond even recalled a time when he was alone in the building and distinctly heard his name called out aloud.

Things didn't stop with weird feeling either. Apparently some of the employees of the business had reported a feeling of being touched by someone, only to discover that no one was there to do the touching. I can only imagine how the poor employee must have felt after that occurrence.

Things even got stranger one day when an employee had nailed a concert flyer to the wall. It seems that the non corporeal inhabitants of the building didn't like the music group. The employee felt a breeze go through the building and went to check on the concert flyer. Well the concert flyer was on the floor; however the expected gash in the paper from it being ripped off the wall by the breeze was not there. Furthermore, the nail that had been used to put the poster up was firmly in the wall. Desmond described that it was like someone had taken the nail out and replaced it.

That wasn't the last occurrence of objects moving on their own volition however. Apparently the unseen occupant of the building believed that everything should be kept in its proper place. I was told that there was at least one instance where the third floor closets had had all the items inside rearranged. Not only that, but the closets were found open. I was told that the closets were always left closed.

[102]

One of the most disturbing things that Desmond told me was of orbs of light that were literally seen floating about the building. He described a blue ball of light that witnesses had seen floating throughout the building. This was reminiscent of sightings that had occurred on what is now referred to as the "Entity" case from the 1970's in which Dr. Barry Taff a renowned parapsychologist and many other investigators observed what Dr. Taff refers to as "Corpuscular Masses of Light" which moved about the room and was witnessed by multiple researchers.

He did not describe the recent "orb" phenomenon where people capture pictures of "orbs of light" on camera when there were no orbs of light to be seen by the naked eye. In recent years the modern "orb" phenomenon has been shown to be nothing more that dust or various other debris, are caught on film and creates a false positive.

While I don't know if the building that housed Sarah and Desmond's in the past is haunted. I definitely can't discount the many stories told to me about the building in regards to my research.

[103]

Perhaps the next shop to take up residence in that building will have some interesting tales to tell.

LITTLE SUNSHINE TRADING COMPANY

One of the greatest things about Ellicott City is that you can find nearly anything along Main Street. The Little Sunshine Trading Company is unique among the shops in Ellicott City because it carries anything that you could want in regards to bringing joy to a baby or small child. You can find any sort of stuffed animal or toy that a toddler or baby could want. They also carry any of the basic items a baby might need such as blankets and bottles.

A stone building has sat upon the property since the early 1800's. I can't say whether the three floor building that is on the site today is the same building, but I can say that it has a structure that is reminiscent of construction from an earlier time.

Much like most shops in Ellicott City, this is not the first store to occupy the space. The property that the Little Sunshine Trading Company currently sits on what was once private homes and a bakery. There has even been a shoe store and a barbershop on the site. These days you can hardly picture a barber pole sitting outside the building, but apparently there was a time when that was a common scene. One of the most recent shops at the location was Stillridge Herb Shop.

I was lucky enough to find an ex employee of the Stillridge Herb Shop and she had some really interesting stories to tell. This ex employee of the shop did not wish for her name to be used in this work, so for the purposes of these stories I shall call

[106]

her Jane Doe (original eh!). Jane first told me about her own personal experiences in the shop.

Jane told me that one of her first paranormal experiences occurred when she was walking on the second floor. While walking, she felt someone approach her from behind and walk past her. To Jane's surprise, there was no one visible that could have bumped into her.

The spectral occupants of the building liked to make their presence known in other ways as well. Jane told me that though no one in the store smoked tobacco products, a distinct cigar smoke smell would waft throughout the store on occasion. That wasn't the scariest occurrence that happened to Jane though. She was working one day and from out of nowhere an object flew off the shelf and whizzed right past her. I was a bit skeptical of this story, but Jane insisted that the object didn't simply fall off the wall, but flew across the room.

Not all of the accounts of paranormal activity were directly experienced by Jane however. Jane told me a story from a time when the building served as a private home. Apparently the former owner would be lying in bed and an unknown force would knock him out of the bed. That wasn't the only story of someone getting accosted by something that was unseen while in bed either. The grandmother of the owner was said to have been lying in her bed, snug as a bug in a rug, when the blankets would start to be pulled off her. Besides objects being flung across a room, this has to be one of the things that would scare me the most! I need to note that these stories of objects being flung across a room and people being knocked out of bed were reported to have occurred on the third floor. Jane told me specifically that she believes that the third floor seems to house a meaner spirit. The first and second floor seem to house a nice and playful ghost.

The last story of paranormal activity in the building was witnessed by another former employee of Stillridge Herb Shop. Jane told me that they once sold wine at the store. The wine was kept in its own display. Well one morning an employee came in and found that all the wine was lying on the floor.

[108]

Just before writing this book, the building in which the old Stillridge Herb Shop had been located was empty. To my pleasure and surprise I discovered recently that the Little Sunshine Trading Company had moved into the building. I chatted with the owners and they were surprised to hear that I had found some ghost stories regarding the building. As of the last time I spoke with the owners, no paranormal activity had been experienced by them. Though I'm sure that they will be keeping their ears and eyes open!

While I can't say that The Little Sunshine Trading Company is haunted. I can say that you will find an awesome place to pick up some children's toys and supplies. So go ahead and visit the shop, check out the cool toys and just be sure to keep your eyes open. Maybe one of those toys might just start moving around on its own.

WIND RIVER

I've mentioned a number of times throughout this book that you can find nearly anything in Ellicott City. Wind River is the place to go to find Designer Clothing. Every time I have walked near this store it is teeming with customers looking to find a new piece of clothing for their wardrobes. I have seen clothing displayed outside the doors on nice days just awaiting a shopper to find that perfect piece of clothing for them. The staff is also perhaps some of the friendliest and most patient folks to deal with.

The building itself was build in the early to mid 1800's. The building is actually one of 2 row-homes. It was used as a private residence for a few years. In the late 1800's a few businesses used the building. The building has housed a shoe store, a bank, a barber shop and a beauty store. More recently a shop called the Nostalgia stop was at the location and now Wind River occupies the space.

While conducting my research I happened upon this little gem in the middle of Ellicott City. When I went into the store the first person that I spoke to was a nice lady named Jen. I of course introduced myself and told her that I was researching ghost stories for a book about Ellicott City. Jen was a bit hesitant to chat about the occurrences at Wind River, but eventually opened up to me a bit.

Jen told me about the employee's struggle with the front door of the store. The employees at the store, need to go outside the door on occasion to wait on a customer or just to catch a breath of fresh air. Well the door of this store seems to enjoy locking on its own. What is worse is that when the employee steps outside, they usually don't have a key. Now I was a little skeptical at first, but Jen assured me that it had happened to many of the employees at the store. She insisted that I speak to an employee named Kelly and gave me her card.

After numerous tries at catching up with Kelly in person, I was finally able to speak with her on the phone. It was a good thing that I reached her via phone too, because she was leaving employment at the store in the near future and probably will be gone by the time this book is published. Speaking with Kelly was worth the wait though.

The first thing that Kelly did was clarify the story about the front door lock. She told me that the door did have a tendency to lock employees outside and that the lock had been changed recently. The phenomenon with the door stopped after that.

Of course not all the paranormal phenomenon stopped. The invisible resident of Wind River has made itself known in other ways. It seems to enjoy turning on the lights after the store is closed for the evening, because employees will come into the store the next day and the lights will be on.

Kelly told me about an event that she witnessed while standing behind the counter one day. There were a number of small trinkets for sale on the counter one day, just sitting there like trinkets tend to do. Suddenly, the trinkets were knocked off the counter by an unseen force. That wasn't the first instance of objects moving on their own volition.

On one occasion the unseen presence in the store made its presence known in a big way. Kelly was in the back of the store when a Metal Arm extender used for hanging clothes in high places removed itself from the ladder it was hanging on and flung itself at her. She was quick enough to dodge the projectile without any physical harm. I was told that the metal arm had actually traveled at a 90 degree angle to get to her. After hearing about this incident I was actually a bit worried. Kelly assured me that an incident such as that one had not happened since.

Whether or not Wind River has a spectral resident is for you to decide. All I that I know is that they have a decent selection of clothing at reasonable prices. Though if you find yourself shopping there one day and ask to have a piece of clothing brought down from on high for your perusal, don't be surprised if an unseen hand gives it to you.

THE WELL

Unfortunately The Well is one of those unique businesses that once made its home in Ellicott City before having to close up shop. It's quite a shame because The Well was definitely a one of the kind place. The Well offered services ranging from yoga, reiki and psychic readings to supplies such as incense and books for those who wished to explore the spiritual side of the world.

The building that housed The Well was pretty hard to research. I could only rely on what I knew of the building from talking to some long time residents of the town. The building once housed an automobile repair shop in the mid 1900's. The building has housed a furniture store and storage for a flower shop in recent years. The Well was the most recent business to occupy the building to date.

I was able to speak with Amy at The Well just before it closed. Amy told me that most of the stories involving the building revolved around a spirit that is known as Al. According to Amy, Al owned the automobile repair shop that was at the location in the mid 1900's. I was able to confirm that there was an automobile repair shop at the location and that the owner did die.

Amy told me that Al has made his presence known in the shop a few different ways. Al seems to have a bit of thief in him. Objects have a habit of disappearing in the store. I guess that Al hasn't taken any money from the store, because I'm sure that would have been reported to the police.

Al has made his presence known in more dramatic ways in the past. Specifically when The Well first opened, Al made a huge and even scary display. The story goes that just before The Well was going to open, one of the employees came into the store and discovered a huge mess. Overnight one of the shelving units had either fallen or been pushed over. The store was locked so the logical assumption would be to say that the shelf had just fallen over. However there were mitigating circumstances so to speak. Along with the shelf being knocked over, there was a glass table that was completely smashed. So either there was a really good burglar that liked breaking into stores just to knock over shelves, smash glass tables, and then leave and relock the door, or Al just wanted to express himself with his new roommates.

After this little temper tantrum, Amy told me that the folks at The Well gave Al the boot. It does seem that their supernatural resident left completely though one has to consider that objects had a tendency to disappear in the store even after the big disturbance.

As a side note, I was told that the area outside of The Well is a hotspot for paranormal activity. Apparently people that have are sensitive seem to sense a presence even outside of the Well.

Of course there is no way to know if Al was the real cause of the havoc that was wrought when The Well opened. We really don't know if Al was the source or if he was banished forever like Amy said. However the building currently sits vacant. We will just have to wait for a new shop to take up residence to know for certain if he is gone, or if he has stuck around eternally watching over his property.

ENVY SALON

Along Old Columbia Pike you will notice a rather striking white house. Should you choose to go inside, you will find a really cool hair salon. The first floor is sort of a waiting and sales area. You can sit down and relax on the velvet antique sofa. If sitting down isn't for you, take a walk around and see the items that are for sale. While I was in there I noticed a cool book on Ellicott City's History. I can't imagine a better thing to read about while getting your hair done in historic Ellicott City, than a book on its past.

The brick building that houses the Envy Salon was built in the mid 1800's. Actually the front portion of the building was constructed in the mid 1800's. It wasn't until the late 1800's that the additions to the building were added to make the building that you see today. The building was a private residence for years. The most recent resident of the location is the Envy Salon.

In my travels throughout Ellicott City, I have always found myself looking at Envy Salon and thinking that the place must have some great stories. In doing my research for this book, I jumped at the opportunity to do some research at the salon. I certainly wasn't surprised when I found out that there were some interesting stories of paranormal activity revolving around Envy Salon. I interviewed the receptionist at the salon and she imparted the stories that she knew to me.

The first story that she told me was about a female entity that has been reported in the building. A few customers have reported to sense a female presence in the building. These customers are supposedly sensitive to the presence of spirits. While

I do believe that there are those who do possess a sixth sense of sorts, I never would admit it as evidence of a haunting. The thing about this story that struck me was that another story corroborates the psychic impressions. According to the receptionist, at least one employee has actually seen a female entity on the third floor of the Salon.

A spectral woman isn't the only person that has been seen or sensed in Envy Salon. An employee was going about her work one day when she looked into a mirror on the second floor. What she saw looking back at her wasn't just her face, but an image of a little boy standing behind her. When she turned around, the boy was gone. I for one get shivers that go up my spine when I think of looking in a mirror and seeing someone looking back that isn't in the room. I can only imagine the employee's fright at seeing that image in the mirror.

At least one stylist has had a close encounter when alone one night. The story is that while closing up the salon one evening, this stylist was walking down the stairs. While doing so, she felt as though someone was following her very closely. Since no one was in the store at the time, there was no explanation for why this feeling occurred.

One of the scariest stories that I heard involving the salon was one that involved the salon manager's husband. Mind you this story is second hand, but the receptionist was very certain of the facts during the retelling. Massages were once offered at the salon, but aren't any longer. This man was lying on the massage table when suddenly he felt a force push him off of the table. I for one would not want to experience being pushed off of a massage table by an unseen force.

[122]

The most popular spirit in the Salon isn't even human. There have been multiple reports from different clients that they have felt a cat brush up against their legs in the store. The customer insists that the store has a cat mascot, but there isn't one to be found. That poor customer has had an encounter with the ghost cat of Envy Salon. There have been children in the salon that have claimed to see a small cat roaming around. However, no adults have reported seeing such an animal.

I cannot say one way, or another that the Envy Salon has spectral residents residing there. I can tell you that one can get their hair styled there by real professionals. Heck you can even enjoy the atmosphere of a truly awesome building with some comfortable antique furniture. My advice is to keep your eyes open and don't be surprised if you catch a glimpse of something out of the ordinary happening during your visit.

Ghosts of Ellicott City by Russ Noratel

THE HOWARD COUNTY HISTORICAL SOCIETY MUSEUM

From Main Street Ellicott city you can look up and see the large spire of what appears to be a Church near the Howard County Courthouse. As you approach this church built of stone, you can observe the old bell tower which lies beneath it's majestic spire. When you get near the church you realize that a parish does not reside within its historic walls. What you will find before you is the Howard County Historical Society Museum. Inside you will find all manner of relics from Howard County's past. You can see everything from old guns and civil war uniforms, to portraits of prominent figures from Ellicott Cities old days.

The building is not the first church building to be located at the site. In the early to mid nineteenth century the First Presbyterian Church was built at the location. By the late 1800's the congregation wanted to expand the building, but tragically the building collapsed during construction. Not being the types to just give up, the Presbyterian congregation decided to build a new church on the site. The second church was constructed with stone from the local quarries and is the same basic building that you see to this day. Eventually the congregation outgrew the

[126]

Presbyterian Church. The building was purchased by Mrs. Alda Hopkins Clark and granted to the Howard County Historical Society. Mrs. Clark donated the Church to the Howard County Historical Society in the name of her late husband, Judge James Clark.

It's a real treat for a history buff like me to go into any historic building or museum. However it's an even bigger treat for that history buff when they are also a paranormal investigator and they hear firsthand accounts of activity in relation to that museum. The Howard County Historical Society Museum is just such a place. I was lucky enough to meet Karen Griffith who is the museum curator and she told me some very interesting stories about The Howard County Historical Society Museum. These stories weren't just about the history of Howard County either!

It seems that Karen has had a few experiences in the museum that she just can't explain. The first incident that she reported to me occurred while she was in the museum basement, where the office is. While sitting there doing paperwork, Karen has heard the sound of footsteps coming from the floor above.

The strange thing is that she knew that the doors were locked and she was the only one in the museum at the time!

It seems that whatever else that inhabits the Howard County Historical Society Museum likes to move around a bit. Karen told me that sometimes when she is closing the museum for the evening, she will turn off all of the lights in the place. At one light switch in particular, she will feel as though someone is standing directly behind her when there isn't anyone that could possibly be standing there.

The most chilling experience that Karen told me about was one that happened when she was sitting at a table on the main floor of the museum. From how I understood her story, she was sitting at this table doing work, when she suddenly felt someone playing with her hair. Karen turned around only to find that no one was there to play with her hair.

A paranormal investigating team was even invited into the location to conduct an investigation. Karen told me that at one point during an audio experiment a team member asked for a sign from whatever was residing in the museum. The response that occurred was in the form of a loud bang originating from an unknown source.

The team returned and revealed some evidence in the form of electronic voice phenomenon (evp) that had been caught during some audio experiments. For those of you not used to the lingo of paranormal investigators, EVP is voices or sounds that are caught on voice recorders that weren't heard by those present at the time of recording. According to Karen, a very light female voice can be heard in the recording that she was presented. Unfortunately I wasn't able to review the recording, but I know that EVP is commonly caught at locations that are suspected to be haunted.

After hearing about all of this activity within museum, I couldn't help but to arrange to investigate the place. During my team's initial investigation, one team member heard a distinct knocking coming from the interior walls. We tried to duplicate the sound through natural means, but could not do so.

During the investigation I spoke with Karen again and she said that the activity had been picking up since my last visit to the site. While sitting in her office in the basement, Karen had placed her purse firmly on the desk to get something out of it. She turned around, and heard a thud. When she turned back around to see what it was, she found her purse sitting upright on the floor. Karen said that the purse had been firmly on the desk, and not teetering on the edge. I gotta say that I believe her story of the purse moving on its own, because if it had fallen off the edge of the table, the contents would have been spilled out and the purse would have been laying on its side. Heck I consulted a few female friends about how the purse would land, and they told me that it would have spilled its contents on the floor. Apparently Murphy 's Law strongly effects purses! In all honesty, having an object move around on its own is one of the most frightening things that could happen to a person.

While we may never know if the Howard County Historical Society Museum is truly haunted, we will be able to see all types of historic artifacts there. While you are there be sure to talk to the curator. She is very knowledgeable in the history of Howard County. And if you are real nice, she might just tell you a few tales of the paranormal that have occurred at the museum, along with her stories about the historic items on display there!

Ghosts of Ellicott City by Russ Noratel

OAK LAWN

One of the most talked about sites in Ellicott City is Oak Lawn Seminary. Not only is it one of the most talked about, it can be easily missed when you are looking for it. You will be pleasantly surprised when you find this large stone building which appears to have been built into the structure of the new Courthouse building. Oak Lawn can be discerned from the courthouse from the iron railings that you will find surrounding the porch.

[133]

Originally built in the mid 1800's this building first housed the Edward Parsons Hayden family. Later the building would become Oak Lawn Seminary, which was private school for girls. This building has also housed the Howard County Board of Education and the County Courthouse. Most recently, the building houses the county law library.

As I said earlier, Oak Lawn is perhaps one of the most talked about haunted locations in Ellicott City. The stories about the haunting of Oak Lawn Seminary have been going on for years. Though I have seen Oak Lawn from the outside on numerous occasions, I have never witnessed paranormal activity. I have heard many stories both in writing and through word of mouth regarding the place.

I will start with the most famous story about Oak Lawn, which would be the famous cooking ghost. Now I know that you are thinking with a name like the "cooking ghost" people have seen a fellow with a chef's hat running around the kitchen of the building. This assumption would be wrong however. When Oak Lawn was occupied by the District Court, employees would report coming to work and smelling that wonderful smell of eggs and bacon cooking. However when they went to look for a nice meal, they would find that nothing was available. The way that I understand it, is that there weren't any cooking appliances whatsoever in the building to make those wonderful smells. Personally I would be disappointed if I came to work, and smelled a nice breakfast cooking, only to find that nothing was actually there for me to eat! The smells were reported to have persisted throughout the day and into the night.

The cooking ghost doesn't just like to cook phantom meals for its guest either. There were reports of a coffee pot that that the spectral chef seemed to enjoy turning on and off. Apparently this ghost was a fan of coffee! The ghostly cook would even go so far as to turn the coffee pot on when it was unplugged. Having an unplugged appliance suddenly turn on by itself has to be one of the most frightening and amazing things that a person could witness.

Oak Lawn's ghosts don't just like to cook phantom meals for the living guests of the building, they enjoy causing a bit of mischief as well. Employees of the building would constantly report that lights would turn on and off by themselves. Mind you this was at a time before automatic light switches that can sense if you are in the room and turn the lights on or off.

People have reported hearing the sounds of footsteps in the building, when no one was there to make those footfalls. While taking its ghostly stroll, the ghost of Oak Lawn likes to ask for company. Some employees reported hearing their names being called out from an unknown source within the building as well.

There have also been sightings of the ghost reported as well. One person saw what appeared to be a man standing in the front of the building one morning. While normally this wouldn't be unusual, the building was locked up and the person was there to open it. After a search of the building for the intruder, no one was found.

I have heard reports of eerie late night encounters with the phantom of Oak Lawn as well.

There was an employee that reportedly worked the night shift in the building. Reportedly the employee witnessed an amazing paranormal display of napkins that folded themselves, and then unfolded themselves in mid air! This employee reportedly saw what they believed was the ghost in the form of a misty white ball that disappeared as quickly as it had appeared.

The legend of Oak Lawn grows with each passing year. It is perhaps one of the most well known haunting in Ellicott City, if not the whole of Maryland. So the next time you are taking a stroll around the Howard County Courthouse, keep an eye out for Oak Lawn. Make sure to keep your nose open as well, for you may be lucky enough to catch the smell of a culinary concoction that the "Cooking Ghost" is preparing just for you!

THE PHOENIX EMPORIUM

As you drive under the railroad bridge coming into Ellicott City, you will notice one of the most well known bars in the town. Before you is a 2 story structure that houses one of the best local watering holes in town, The Phoenix Emporium. Locals around the town know that the Phoenix Emporium is one of the best places to go to find food and spirits. The bar is stocked with many different micro brews and various liquors to suit you pallet. You can get some really great food there as well. In my opinion this is the place to go if you want a cheeseburger, trust me! It isn't just the food that is great either. The place just has a really cool feel to it. As you sit at your table waiting for your delicious meal, you can gaze upon the antique stained glass facades that hang from the ceiling. These stained glass pieces of art were once securely placed over the doors of homes from within Baltimore city, most with their address numbers clearly visible. It's really quite a sight.

The building isn't the oldest in town by a long shot. Throughout most of the 1800's the lot was part of a lumber yard. In the late 1800's a one story grocery store was on the site. In the early 1900's a second story was added to the structure. The building has housed many bars and restaurants over the years. The most recent tenant is the Phoenix Emporium, which has become one of the most well known bar and restaurant in Ellicott City. The Phoenix Emporium was established in 1978.

Of course "The Phoenix" as the locals lovingly call it, may have patrons from beyond this world.

There have been many reports of paranormal activity at this pub for years. If you ask pretty much anyone in town about haunted places, they will point you to the Phoenix.

During my research I was able to speak with a couple of the Phoenix employees. Most notable among these employees was Dawn, a waitress/bartender at the establishment. Boy did she have some stories to tell!

Dawn started off by telling me of her own experiences at the Phoenix. While working one day, she told me that she clearly heard someone say directly to her Hey, how are you. She turned around to answer and no one was there to have done the speaking. It's heartwarming to know that whoever may be haunting the Phoenix genuinely cares about how you are feeling.

One of the scarier experiences that Dawn told me about involved the kitchen. According to Dawn, she was walking out of the kitchen when she heard the crash of plates hitting the floor. She turned around to see these plates falling to the floor. While

[140]

falling plates may are not uncommon in a restaurant, these plates were secure only moments before and there was no way that they fell on their own. It was almost as if a spectral hand had pushed the plates down.

There have been other employees at the Phoenix that have experienced strange happenings. Late at night, many folks have reported a strange and eerie feeling in building. There have been multiple reports from employees who have heard voices, even after the bar has closed. Stranger yet are the reports of employees catching glimpse of people walking in rooms, only to go and discover that no one is there! The best story that I heard was of a civil war soldier that was spotted in the basement of the building. The same apparition was witnessed by at least 2 separate waitresses.

I was told of a more recent experience that occurred right in front of a bar patron. There is a tip bucket that hangs above the bar on the second floor of the building. Before the very eyes of one of the regular patrons, this bucket began swinging violently on its own. I guess the ghost just wanted it's share of the tips. This was enough evidence of the paranormal for that patron because they left the bar scared out of their mind! The employees that witnessed this phenomenon were intrigued, and did not run. From what I was told, there was not a natural explanation for the movement of the bucket. I had heard about a former employee of the Phoenix that refused to go to the second floor own her own. Perhaps she witnessed something similar to the bucket moving on its own!

The Phoenix Emporium is a place that you need to go to when visiting Ellicott City. The Phoenix has a great atmosphere. You can get great food and there are a large variety of drinks to choose from. Of course while you are eating and drinking, keep an eye out, because one of the phantoms of the Phoenix might be eating and drinking with you!

THE WINE BIN: FORMERLY THE ELLICOTT CITY FIRE STATION

Historic Ellicott City has experienced its share of tragedy over the years. This tragedy came in many forms, including fires. These fires would need to be fought and lives needed to be saved. The heroic people that would do this job were the members of the Fire Department. The first Volunteer Fire Company was formed in 1888. These volunteers not only volunteered to be the town fire fighters, but also donated their time to building the first Ellicott City Fire Station which is now a museum.

Many firefighters over the years have spent time in the Ellicott City Fire Station. This building was completed in 1939 for the Fire Fighters of Ellicott City. Unlike the 2 previous Fire Stations that only housed equipment, or at most the Fire Captain and Equipment, this one would be able to house the firefighters and their equipment. In 1998, the fire company moved to a brand new, state of the art fire station on Montgomery Road.

Since the move, the Ellicott City Fire Station has housed an Art Gallery and a government agency. Most recently The Wine Bin has taken up residence on the first floor of the building. The Wine Bin offers up a wide array of wine to those who enjoy it. They even offer a few Firefighter inspired wines as well. Of course the spirits offered for sale at The Wine Bin may not be the only ones present in the old Fire Station.

In order to seek out some first-hand accounts I tracked down a fire fighter that had served at the old Fire Station. Luckily I was able to find one such fire fighter, though I had to promise to keep their identity out of the book as a condition of them telling me their chilling stories. For the purposes of telling these stories, I will call my source "Jo".

Jo told me that the firefighters believed that the spirit of Mr. Harry was haunting the Ellicott City Fire Station. Mr. Harry was Captain Harry Shiply that served at the station. Jo told me that it was believed that Mr. Harry died at the Fire Station, but I was unable to confirm that. I was able to confirm that 2 firefighters who served at the Fire Station died tragically in the line of duty in the 1950's.

According to Jo, firefighters at the station would hear the sounds of footsteps going up the steps of the firehouse. Most of them believed that it was Mr. Harry walking the halls of the station for which he once served. Of course phantom footsteps were not the only experiences to be had at the station.

One such firefighter would not spend any time alone in the station. Specifically, there would be instances where three firefighters would be on duty. Two would go out on a medical call, leaving one at the station. Well this firefighter would claim to hear footsteps inside the station when no one was around to make them. So he would take a chair and the station dog named Yogi and sits outside and waits until his comrades came back.

Good old Yogi the dog was also affected by the haunting. Many firefighters witnessed Yogi become very agitated for no apparent reason. Jo told me that it seemed as though Yogi was sensing a presence in the location. Of course Yogi would never be able to tell us his side of the story because dogs can't talk! Of course there have been many reports of dogs and other animals having agitated reactions to reportedly haunted locations.

Jo had some experiences in the fire station as well. Jo remembered leaving rooms at the fire station and turning the lights off. Suddenly the lights would come back on. Not surprising, this would startle Jo. This event didn't occur just once however. It happened a number of times. Jo also had experiences in the restroom. Apparently Mr. Harry was a fan of the restrooms because he would turn on the faucets while Jo was inside.

[147]

According to the folks at The Wine Bin, there hasn't been much in the way of activity lately. Of course that doesn't mean that the spirits of the Ellicott City Fire Station have left. They may simply be getting used to their new housemates at The Wine Bin. Whether or not you believe in ghosts, I suggest stopping in to check out the fine wines sold at this store if you are over 21 that is. Just remember, while looking at the many spirits sold there, if you hear the sounds of someone walking behind you, it might just be the ghost of Mr. Harry trying to say hello!

HOWARD
COUNTY
TOURISM
OFFICE

The first place that a person visits when going to a new town is the local tourism office. Luckily, visitors to Ellicott City have an easy trek to the tourism office since Howard County Tourism's office is right off Main Street next to a huge public parking lot. The office is located in the same building as the now closed Ellicott City Post Office.

Originally, there were wood framed structures on the property in which the Howard County Tourism office and Post Office building now reside. This wood framed structure held the Hillsinger Funeral Home up until the 1930's. The funeral home was demolished and the Post Office building was constructed. The post office was open until September of 2008 and now stands vacant. Howard County Tourism's office is located on the side of the building on the way from Main Street to the parking lot.

You can find all kinds of information regarding the best spots to visit from the nice folks at Howard County Tourism. They even run tours from that office, including ghost tours of Ellicott City. The funny thing is that their ghost stories begin at their home office. I was lucky enough to sit down with Ed Lilley at Howard County Tourism to hear his tales of the supernatural. During the interview, Ed told me about a number of incidents that have occurred to him and his fellow employees at the Tourism office.

[150]

The first story that Ed told me was of an interview that he did for a student regarding a class project. This student set up a video camera on a table in the meeting room of the office and proceeded with the interview. Upon review of the tape, the picture was in motion. Ed told me that no one had touched the table on which the camera was sitting during the interview, but the video clearly showed movement.

Phantom smells have been reported in the office as well. Ed reported that he had smelled the scent of flowers, much like one would smell in a funeral home. He told me that the smell originated in the hall and meeting room. At least 3 other people have reported that very same smell at different times.

In one of the storage rooms, doors would rattle for no apparent reason. The employees would go to investigate but the rattling would have stopped. Shortly afterward a thumping sound would be heard.

One incident that occurred involved a copy room which gets locked up at night. Ed came in one

[151]

morning and unlocked the door to this copy room to see a strange sight. He saw the shelving that was attached to the wall on one end of the room, now across the room along with the items that were on it. The shelving had been flung by some unknown force over the course of the night in a locked room.

There have also been incidents in the office that employees other than Ed have experienced. Employees have reported feeling extremely cold spots in the building.   There have even been reports of hearing the sound of footsteps and objects being moved in the post office above the Tourism office, when the post office was closed!

While these incidents are pretty impressive, there have been a number of jaw-dropping incidents that Ed was kind enough to tell me about. At least twice, an apparition of a woman has been sighted by either Ed, or another employee.

Ed's sighting of the ghost; the employees lovingly call Louisa, occurred one day while he was sitting at his desk in the office. He peered over the counter and saw a woman standing there in a long dress. Ed described this dress as being one that would have been worn by a woman in the 1800's. He was only able to observe the upper portion of the woman's body during his experience. Apparently it was kind of difficult to discern Louisa's age, but he thinks that she would have been around 30 years old. Like most apparition sightings, Louisa was gone as fast as she arrived.

Another employee, Vicky, has caught a glimpse of Louisa as well. Vicky's office is in the back portion of the Tourism office. As she was sitting at her desk one day, she observed a woman walking through the hallway and out of sight. Vicky told me that sighting was quick and she was unable to get a good description of the apparition. She was certain however that she had not just seen a customer walking through the hallway.

Whether or not you believe in ghosts, I would suggest visiting the Howard County Tourism office on any visit to Ellicott City. They have a plethora of information regarding Ellicott City and Howard County. While you are there, ask them about the ghost stories regarding their building. You also might want to consider reserving a spot on their ghost tour of Ellicott City. It is an extremely popular tour to take and I am certain that you won't be disappointed! Just beware, during your visit, there might be a woman standing in the corner dressed in the clothing from a different era. Don't fret; it's just Louisa saying hello!

THE LEGEND OF SEVEN HILLS ROAD

Most people have heard of that little republic/empire that lasted for about a thousand years and was the biggest in the known world that will forever be known as Rome. Would it surprise you if I told you that Rome and Ellicott City have something in common? Well they do have something in common. The city of Rome was surrounded by seven hills and Ellicott City is also surrounded by seven hills. Pretty cool story, eh?

Over the years, the legend of the Demon Car of Seven Hills Road has been passed down through the years. No, this legend has nothing to do with the Seven Hills of Rome and a demonic car that travels the roads around them. This legend has been around since the mid 1900's.

According to the legend, if you drive on College Avenue, also known as Seven Hills Road, you don't want to hit the seventh hill at midnight. If you hit that seventh hill at midnight, a demonic car, with headlights blazing with hellfire will chase you down. I've never met someone that was chased by the demon car, so that means that either very few people have seen it, or very few have lived to talk about it.

This author is not brave enough to trek out to College Avenue at midnight, but not for the reasons that you believe. I mainly don't want to drive that road at night because it is very windy and dark. My curiosity did get the best of me one afternoon day though and I drove down the road. After hitting the "seventh" hill, I did have a weird experience. A really big vulture popped out of the woods which surround the road and flew in front of my car for about one hundred feet. It was really an amazing site. I have to tell you that even during the day; this road can be pretty dark, with some of the road being surrounded by woods.

Ellicott City is a really beautiful place and I really enjoy the woodland surroundings. I still don't recommend taking a trip down Seven Hills Road looking for the Demon Car of legend. For one, would you really want to encounter it and secondly, do you really want a demon car chasing you down and ultra windy and dark road? Personally I wouldn't want to have to get in any type of situation where I was being chased down that road!

BIBLIOGRAPHY AND WORKS CITED

Okonowitz, Ed.   Haunted Maryland: Ghosts and Strange Phenomena of the Old Line State.   Mechanicsburg, PA: Stackpole Books, 2007

Gramm, Joetta.   Historic Ellicott City: A Walking Tour. Woodbine, MD: K&D Limited Inc,1996

Back, Mollie and Wolle, Brian. Ghost Encounters: Tales of the Supernatural Residents of Historic Ellicott City. Gettysburg, PA: Unicorn Press, 1998

Trevillian, Bob and Carter, Frank. Treasure on the Chesapeake Bay. Glen Burnie, MD: Spyglass Enterprises, 1983

Wilson, Vince. The Haunted Field Guide Series: Ghost Science: The Essential Guide to the Scientific Study of Ghosts & Hauntings. Decatur, Illinois: Whitechapel Productions Press, 2006

Guiley, Rosemary Ellen.   The Encyclopedia of Ghosts and Spirits. Second Edition. New York, NY: Checkmark Books, An imprint of Facts on File Inc, 2000

Goeller, Victoria and Kusterer, Janet. <u>Then & Now: Ellicott City.</u> Charlestone, SC, Chicago, IL, Portsmouth, NH, San Francisco, CA: Arcadia Publishing, 2006

Goeller, Victoria and Kusterer, Janet. <u>Remembering Ellicott City: Stories From the Patapsco River Valley.</u> Charleston, SC: The History Press, 2009

Gallagher, Trish. <u>Ghosts & Haunted Houses of Maryland.</u> Centreville, MD: Tidewater Publishers, 2007.

Taylor, Troy, <u>The Ghost Hunters Guidebook: The Essential Guide to Investigating Ghosts & Hauntings.</u> Third Edition. Alton, Illinois: Whitechapel Productions Press, A Division of the History & Hauntings Book Co. 2004

Wilson, Vince. <u>Ultimate Ghost Hunter: The Handbook for the Amateur Parapsychologist.</u> Cosmic Pantheon Press 2009

Noratel, Russ. <u>Ellicott City's Guide to Haunted Places.</u> Cosmic Pantheon Press 2008

[159]

ONLINE
SOURCES

Ellicott City Graphic Arts. 2004-2008. Welcome to Ellicott City, in Maryland. Retrieved September 4, 2008 www.ellicottcity.net

Ellicott City Maryland, Wikipedia: The Free Encyclopedia. Last modified September 9, 2008. Retrieved September 14, 2008. http://en.wikipedia.org/wiki/Ellicott's_Mills,_Maryland

Haunted Ellicott City, Ghosts of the Prairie. Troy Taylor 1998. Retrieved September 6, 2008 www.prairieghosts.com/hauntelcity.html

"harveyonline2525 ." You Tube: Broadcast Yourself. November 6, 2007. Spirits in an Ellicott City Restaurant. Retrieved September 6, 2008

http://www.youtube.com/watch?v=RB4xHHoR9bw

Cacao Lane Restaurant, Retrieved January 31, 2010 www.cacaolane.net

The Baltimore Society for Pranormal Researh

www.bsprnet.com

ARTICLES

McIlory, Megan. "Ellicott City: Hotbed for the Paranormal" The Baltimore Examiner (October 30, 2006).

Shayne, Jennifer Siciliano. "Ellicott City" The Baltimore Sun (January 14, 2000).

Schleicher, Brad. "Insiders Guide to Historic Ellicott City" The Baltimore Sun, (October 28.2007)

Martini, Kelly. "Ellicott City Hosts 'Haunted' History Walks" Maryland Newsline (November 1, 2007)

Quinn, Carolyn. " Dare to take the Ellicott City Ghost Tour"Mid-Atlantic Travel Destinations: Trips & Getaways (September/October 2007)

Taff, Dr. Barry E. "The Real Life Entity Case" PSI Journal Of Investigative Psychical Research Vol. 4(1) pp.9-26 (2008)

SPECIAL THANKS

I wish to extend my very special thanks to the people at the Howard County Historical Society for their guidance in my search for information on the history of Ellicott City. My heartfelt thanks goes out to Karen Griffith for taking time out of her schedule to answer my questions about the Howard County Historical Society Museum and being an excellent resource for my historical research about Ellicott City. I would also like to thank Ed Lilley at Howard County Tourism Inc. for sitting down for an interview. Lastly I'd like to take the time to thank each and every person who took the time to talk with me about their stories of paranormal activity around Ellicott City. It has truly been a pleasure speaking with you all and being able to write down these great stories.

ABOUT THE AUTHOR

Russ has always had an interest in stories of ghosts and the paranormal

since a very early age. He became increasingly interested in the paranormal in his mid 20's, when he realized that others were conducting scientific research in the field. Since getting into the field in late 2005, he has been on dozens of investigations and worked numerous cases. In early 2008 Russ joined the Baltimore Society for Paranormal Research. Russ eventually took over leadership of the organization in September 2009 from its longtime leader Vince Wilson.

Now, Russ educates those who wish to learn about paranormal research and investigation by offering training workshops and lecturing at conferences. He appeared in a training video on paranormal investigation for MonkeySee.com in 2008. Russ has been interviewed by local television and radio shows regarding paranormal research. He has written articles for Ghost Tech Magazine and various publications online. His first book titled **Ellicott City's Guide to Haunted Places**, which was released in December 2008.

COSMIC PANTHEON PRESS

Cosmic Pantheon Press - the publishing company for the next generation of authors

Books from Cosmic Pantheon Press and its writers are focused on the spiritual and scientific future of humankind while simultaneously visiting our past for the purpose of intellectual enlightenment.

Titles from Cosmic Pantheon Press focus on everything from American and World History to some of the *mysteries* of nature including the paranormal and supernatural.

HISTORY
Read about great people and places.

Explore mo. Are you one of our future writers? Visit the CONTACT US section of our site and find out! We are looking forward to hearing from you!

www.cosmicpantheon.com

CPSIA information can be obtained at www.ICGtesting.com
Printed in the USA
BVOW010423140512

289981BV00006B/1/P

9 780983 436942